MW01244371

The Retirement Roadmap

3 Steps to Living Your Best Life

Calvin Goetz

David Riley

Clay Netherlin

The Retirement Roadmap

Copyright © 2017, Calvin Goetz

Published in the United States of America

ISBN: 9781793813930

No parts of this publication may be reproduced without correct attribution
to the author of this book.

Here's What's Inside...

Disclosure

Information contained in this book is for informational purposes only. It is not intended to provide any investment, tax or legal advice or provide the basis for any financial decisions. Be sure to speak to a qualified tax, legal and financial professional before making any decisions about your personal situation. Strategy Financial Group is not associated with, or endorsed by, the U.S. government or any governmental agency. Please consult with the Social Security Administration for guidance on your individual situation. All statements in this material referring to protections and guarantees are referencing benefits for Fixed Index Annuities and/or Life Insurance products, which are backed by the financial strength and claims-paying ability of the issuing insurer. Investment advice is offered through Strategy Financial Services, LLC, a Registered Investment Adviser in the state of Arizona. Strategy Financial Services, LLC, may only transact business in states in which it is registered, or in which it is excluded or exempted from registration. Such registration does not imply any level of skill or training. Insurance and annuity products are offered separately through Strategy Financial Insurance, LLC.

Your Road to Retirement!

When I was 6 years old, my dad, Gary, took me to work with him for the first time, and I learned the most valuable lesson of my life. You see, growing up, my dad got up each day at 4 a.m., including most Saturdays, to go to work. He was a construction foreman for one of the largest commercial builders in southern Arizona. He built schools, hospitals, shopping malls; you name it.

When he would come home, he spent hours at night studying large rolls of plans to make sure his crew executed the project correctly the next day. He loved his job, and he worked harder than anyone I know today.

But on Sundays, he liked to relax, and his idea of relaxing was to play music at the crack of dawn on Sunday morning, usually around 7 a.m. At the time, I hated it because all I wanted to do was sleep in, but he played the music way too loud. He loved to play classic country music like Hank Williams and Loretta Lynn. One of his favorites was a guy named Johnny Horton, and one of his favorite Johnny Horton songs was "*North to Alaska.*"

In 2008, my dad lost his job unexpectedly, and I knew that was my chance to step up and be the man he raised me to be. When the financial crisis began in 2008, the construction industry was hit first. My dad's company began laying off workers, and over the course of several months, they went from 40 employees down to four, and then they went out of business.

My dad found himself in an extremely difficult place. He was 62 years old, he had a company truck that would have to be returned, he had no pension and no severance. And, he was unable to find any work. His body had been broken down from years of hard labor and long hours. I watched as my dad lapsed into a depression. This was not what he had planned on. He wanted to work until at least age 65. He wanted to finish paying off his home. Now he had to consider buying a vehicle with no steady income.

At this point in my career, I was starting to have success, and I knew this was my chance to be there for my dad the way he had always been there for me. I started saving extra money each month, and after six months, I had enough for a down payment on a new truck. I drove to the dealership and found a white Toyota Tundra pick-up truck just like my dad's old work truck. It was a base model, but I knew I could afford it. I made the deal and parked that white truck in my driveway. I went to a local craft store and bought the biggest red bow I could find and slapped it right on the hood of that white truck.

I called my mom and dad the next morning and invited them to drive up from Tucson and stay the night with me. They agreed, but when they pulled into the driveway, my dad didn't get it right way. He asked, "whose truck is this?"

I looked at him, smiled, and pulled the keys slowly out of my pocket. "It's yours." He looked at me with confusion and disbelief for a moment, and I said, "come on, get in."

He reached for the door and got in. Then, as he placed the key in the ignition and turned it on, the engine roared to life, and the sound over the speakers started playing Johnny Horton's "*North to Alaska*" at max volume, just the way he always liked it on those Sunday mornings.

I'll never forget that day. I saw my dad smile in a way he hadn't in months. As you get older, you realize your parents are just people too.

I saw what happened to my parents when it came to retirement planning, and I never want any of my clients to be without a plan. I don't want to see anyone I know struggle like my parents did when they decided to retire and didn't have anyone they trusted to explain the concepts of financial planning, wealth management, and taxes. They didn't have anyone in their corner to guide them in ensuring they had a proper savings plan and distribution plan for retirement. Because of what my parents went through, I try to teach and treat each new client as if they were my own mom and dad.

One of the things I'm going to cover in this book is why you want to find a qualified financial advisor; somebody who can help you with a retirement income analysis and build a robust plan for your retirement. There's a lot of information out there. Anybody can search the Internet and read different articles from different points of view, but rarely does somebody sit down with a qualified advisor who can discuss income planning, investment planning, tax planning, long-term healthcare planning, and estate planning all in one setting, and have a team of professionals and referral sources to guide them in the right direction through those topics.

In this book, I'll take you through the same material I share with my clients in my workshops and show you what my Retirement Roadmap 3-Step Review process is. I will give you tips on how to select and choose a good advisor, including what questions to ask, and give you guidance about the main concepts you'll deal with throughout the retirement planning process that you may not have thought of.

I'm going to make a promise to you: when you meet with me and my team, we will give everything we have to make sure you have what we believe to be the right plan in place and are making the right choices for your retirement. I learned from my dad the only thing we are really in control of is how much we give of ourselves. He taught me that the very first day he took me to the jobsite when I was 6 years old.

Enjoy the book!

I hope this book educates you on the reason you want to find a financial professional to partner with you and help you make the right decisions for your retirement planning. I hope this book inspires you to take the time to sit down with a professional and go through your retirement plan, ensuring you're on the right track and nothing is being overlooked. Those who think they have a good handle on everything probably need coaching and guidance the most because they're at the highest risk of making a silly mistake costing them thousands of dollars, because they think they already know it all.

To Your Retirement Success!

Calvin Goetz

10 Keys to Planning and Living Your Best Retirement

Baby Boomers have changed every aspect of life they have touched, and retirement is no different. They are reinventing retirement. They want more for their retirement than their parents had. They want to be able to travel to see family and the world, and they want to pursue passions they put off while they raised their families. To achieve those goals, they need to have a solid financial footing so they can live their best retirement.

Most of this book offers my views about how to create and preserve your wealth, enabling you to live a retirement you are proud of. My *10 Keys to Planning and Living Your Best Retirement* focus on some of the aspects of retirement beyond the financial. Having peace of mind about your financial future is only one part of a successful retirement.

Have a sense of purpose and meaning. Make every day meaningful. Oxford University suggests a meaningful life lessens the effects of aging, and research from Patrick Hill and Nicholas Turiano found people who have a sense of purpose or direction in life outlive their peers. In fact, people with a sense of purpose had a 15% lower risk of death, compared with those who said they were more or less aimless[1].

According to the research, it doesn't seem to matter when people find their direction. It could be in their 20s, 50s, or 70s, even when controlled for other factors that affect longevity like age, gender, and emotional well-being. The study found that a sense of purpose led to a longer life.

Make the best of it. Accepting the realities of aging and making the best of whatever life throws in your path is the best mindset with which to approach your retirement. A sense of humor doesn't hurt either!

Take it easy on yourself. Give yourself permission to make mistakes—because you will. Don't feel guilty if you spend some time just doing nothing. Instead, enjoy your good fortune at just being retired.

Take a chance. Approach retirement with a goal of trying something new. Step out of your comfort zone. Keep learning. It's a key to staying young.

Be frugal. Try to live below your means, since it is highly likely you will encounter unexpected expenses at some time during your retirement.

Just do it. Strive for a good balance between relaxation and activity. Too much of either doesn't usually work out too well.

Live in the now. None of us knows for certain how much time we have. Don't let planning be the enemy of doing.

Live with no regrets. Make amends, clear the air, and do what is necessary so you have no regrets haunting your retirement years.

Pursue a passion. When you were working, you likely dreamed of following your passion in some area. Retirement gives you the opportunity to do that. Don't waste it.

Put family first. Research shows retirees with rich family lives enjoy their retirements much more, so spend some of the extra time you have fostering any neglected relationships and being there for family and friends.

Disclosed and Undisclosed Fees + Costs

One of the most important things I can do when sitting down with a new client is help them do a fee analysis on their existing holdings to find out exactly what they're paying and how it's impacting their overall plan.

You probably go grocery shopping. As you walk through the grocery store, picking different items off the shelves, you look at the price of the items and put them in the cart. Subconsciously, you're adding up the cost of each of the items you've placed in the shopping cart as you go through your routine at the grocery store.

When you get to the checkout aisle, you put everything on the belt, and the price appears for each item. At the end, the cashier says, "Your total is $100," but you probably already had a pretty good idea of what that number would be based on your estimate.

Often, people don't sit down to review the costs of all their different investments, get a real total, and then equate that back from a percentage into actual dollars and cents.

One of the largest studies to date on fees and expenses for mutual funds was done by the professors of finance at UC Davis over 10 years ago[2]. They found that mutual funds have two different sets of fees: disclosed fees, including the advisory fee and expense ratio, and undisclosed fees, including turnover cost, transaction expenses, bid-ask spread, and 12b-1 fees inside the mutual fund.

When they added all these fees up, they found, on average, between 3% and 5% of the overall value of the account was taken up by fees and expenses. Yet, when they surveyed people entering retirement about their cost expectations for funds, most people thought they were paying half that amount.

When you take your shopping cart up to the cashier, you don't want to see a total that's double what you thought you would pay. Going through an independent risk and fee analysis with a qualified advisor is one of the first steps to getting control over how much money you're paying and to keeping more money in your pocket in order to sustain your retirement lifestyle for as long as possible.

What Makes Strategy Financial Group Standout

The point is, most people don't have a process. They don't have a set of questions to ask or somebody qualified to do a review of all their different account statements with all their different custodians: 401(k)s, IRAs, Roth IRAs, 403(b)s, brokerage accounts. They don't have somebody who takes the time to do an analysis to see exactly what's being charged in fees and expenses, get a handle on that, and redirect more of that money back into their pockets. I believe that's what makes Strategy Financial Group different: we believe in helping you understand all the critical facts necessary to make sound financial decisions for your future.

I am an American success story. I was born in Tucson, AZ and went to college in Flagstaff. I built this business from the ground up. I have a team of advisors and access to our referral partners: estate planning attorneys, a CPA, and a Medicare specialist. We have built this team of professionals to provide support for all the areas of retirement planning you will face in the future, including income planning, drafting out a written retirement income plan, investment planning, choosing the right investments based on your risk level, and reducing fees and expenses on those investments wherever possible.

Tax planning involves minimizing taxes you'll pay in the future; figuring out ways to structure assets in the right buckets so you can pass the assets to your heirs in a more tax-efficient way. Healthcare planning includes Medicare supplement or Medicare advantage discussions and long-term care concerns. Finally, estate planning involves working with a qualified estate planning attorney to make sure all of the assets are titled properly and beneficiary forms are filled out properly to avoid any tax issues or mistakes in the event of incapacity or death.

We have five locations in Arizona. Our primary office is at 3200 E. Camelback Road, Suite 285, Phoenix, AZ 85018. We also have locations in Chandler, Scottsdale, Oro Valley and Tucson.

When you meet with me or one of the other qualified advisors at my firm, you'll go through our Retirement Roadmap 3-Step Review process. This includes reviewing your tax return and estate plan, doing a complete retirement income analysis, and doing a risk and fee analysis to make sure you have the right allocation for your retirement plan. We'll also look for ways to minimize those fees and expenses. The process is one of discovery. Based on our meetings, we're able to deliver recommendations for how you can improve what you're currently doing.

Retirement Roadmap
3-Step Review

Step 1: 1040 Tax Return Review

When I was growing up, my mom and dad could never agree on where to invest money. My mom was more of a risk-taker, and she wanted to buy individual stock. My dad didn't like risk. He liked money at the bank or under the mattress. Years ago, I walked them through an example to show them where they should invest money if they were going to buy individual stock. The question I asked them was: should you buy individual stock inside your IRA or outside your IRA?

Here's an example: let's say you had $200,000 inside your IRA, and you were to buy Kodak. Kodak went bankrupt, so that stock would be worth nothing. If you lost $200,000 inside your IRA, how much of that loss would you be able to write off? The answer is none because you can't write off losses inside your IRA, with rare exception. Had you purchased that stock for Kodak outside your IRA in a brokerage account, you'd be able to write off 100% of the $200,000 loss at a rate of $3,000 a year. That's called a capital loss carry forward.

Let's say you purchased Apple inside your IRA, and your $200,000 turned into $1 million. If you want to sell any of that Apple stock and take a distribution from the IRA, what type of tax will you pay? You will pay ordinary income tax, which, for many retirees, may be higher than long-term capital gains tax rates.

Let's also say that stock was in my dad's IRA, and my dad passed away, leaving the IRA to my mom. As a spousal beneficiary, my mom inherits the $1 million of Apple stock. If she wants to sell any of it and take a distribution, what type of tax will she pay? She'll pay ordinary income tax because, again, it's coming from an IRA, which became her IRA. If my mom dies and leaves all the stock to me, I will have to pay ordinary income tax as I take distributions as well.

Let's flip that scenario around to illustrate the power of owning assets in the right tax bucket. Let's say I had $200,000 in a brokerage account and purchased Apple stock with it. That $200,000 turned into $1 million, and my dad wanted to sell some of it. Assuming he had owned it for at least one year, he will pay long-term capital gains tax rates. What most people don't realize is that if a married couple's taxable income falls below the 25% tax bracket, which is around $75,000 and would include my mom and dad, the long-term capital gains tax rate is zero, as of the time I am writing this book.

If my dad dies, and my mom inherits that $1 million in stock, what happens if it's in a brokerage account in a community property state? The answer is the value of the stock is stepped up from the original cost basis of

$200,000 to the $1 million date-of-death value. My mother does not have to pay any capital gains on the appreciation of that stock over the years. If my mom chooses to keep it, and the stock grows from $1 million to $1.5 million, if she left it all to me upon her death, I would again receive a full step up in a community property state from $1 million to $1.5 million, and would not pay any capital gains taxes on the appreciation of that stock.

What kind of difference does this make? If my dad dies and leaves the IRA to my mom for $1 million and my mom liquidates the IRA, she would pay approximately one-third in taxes or about $333,000 on the $1 million of stock in the IRA. On the other hand, if my dad dies with the Apple stock that's outside the IRA, my mom would receive the full step up from $200,000— the original cost basis—to the current value of $1 million, and she would liquidate all of it and have no capital gains tax on it at all. That is more than $300,000 difference in taxability simply by structuring the asset in the right bucket.

When I had this discussion with my mom and dad years ago, they chose to structure the purchase of individual stock outside their IRAs for all the tax benefits just illustrated.

When you meet with our team, we will review your tax return and figure out if any interest, dividends, or capital gains are hitting page one of your return for things you don't actually need for current income and help you reposition or keep those assets in the right bucket.

The largest demographic in American history is the Baby Boomers. They include anybody born between 1946 (my dad was born in September 1946) and 1964. That's an 18-year period of time encompassing more than 80 million people. Estimates are 10,000 people turn 70 years old every day, starting January 1, 2016.

One of the largest investment portfolios most retirees have is their IRA[3]. This means they worked for an employer for years and rolled that money over to their own IRA. At the age of 70.5, the IRS has some special rules that kick in regarding required minimum distributions. Let me give you an example of two Baby Boomers who are leading the way on this.

Both Presidents Donald Trump and Bill Clinton turned 70 in 2016. They were both born in 1946 and are in the first group of Baby Boomers subject to the 70.5 required minimum distribution (RMD) rules, assuming they both have retirement accounts. President Trump's date of birth is June 14, 1946. President Clinton's date of birth is August 19, 1946. Their dates of birth are just two months apart, but drastically different rules apply to each of them with regards to minimum distributions.

President Trump turned 70.5 in 2016, while Bill Clinton turned 70.5 in 2017, so they each have a different required beginning date (RBD).

Trump's RBD is April 1, 2017, while Clinton's RBD is April 1, 2018. Trump's first required distribution is in 2016, while Clinton's first required distribution is in 2017.

Even calculating how their minimum distribution payment is generated is different for both presidents. Trump will calculate his first RMD using the IRA balance as of Dec. 31, 2015. Clinton will use the Dec. 31, 2016 IRA balance, since his first required minimum distribution is in 2017 because he did not turn 70.5 until 2017.

Even the life expectancies they use will be different. The Internal Revenue Service has two primary life expectancy tables that are used for calculating minimum distributions. Assuming Trump's beneficiary is his wife, Melania, he can use the joint life expectancy table, since Melania is more than 10 years younger than him. Melania Trump was born on April 26, 1970, so in Donald Trump's first RMD year of 2016, she was 46 years old, and he was 70. Trump can use the joint life expectancy table from IRS publication 590-B. The joint life expectancy table for those two ages gives him a divisor factor or life expectancy factor of 38.6.

Trump would then divide his Dec. 31, 2015 IRA balance by 38.6 to arrive at his first RMD. The following year, he would return to that same joint life expectancy table and use the ages for 71 and 47, and so on for each year.

Bill Clinton, on the other hand, would use a more traditional table regardless of who he named as his IRA beneficiary. The joint life expectancy table exception only applies when a spouse who is more than 10 years younger is the beneficiary. Clinton would use the standard uniform lifetime table and look up the factor for age 71, since, unlike Trump, Clinton turned 71 in his first year of distribution: 2017. That factor is 26.5, as opposed to the 38.6 Trump uses.

Let's say each president has a $1 million IRA balance at the end of their respective calendar years. Trump's first RMD will be $25,907, which is $1 million divided by 38.6 years. Bill Clinton's first RMD will be $37,736, which is $1 million divided by 26.5 years. Even though the two men are only 2 months apart in age, Trump's first RMD is $11,829 lower than Clinton's, not only because they turned age 70.5 in different years but also because Trump qualifies to use the joint life expectancy table since his spouse is younger than him by more than 10 years. This saves Trump $11,829 in the first year.

You can see that the RMD rules for a Baby Boomer turning 70.5 and going forward in retirement can be complex and can also have significant consequences even if their birthday is only a few months apart from someone else's. This is why working with an advisor who specializes in retirement planning and understands IRA distribution laws and tax laws related to IRA distribution is so important.

This is also one area where the tax penalties are some of the highest out there if you make a mistake. For example, if Bill Clinton did not process the required minimum distribution of $37,736, the tax penalty would be 50% of that amount, or just over $18,000.

The point is most people don't have a process. They don't have a set of questions to ask. They don't have somebody qualified to take them through their questions and help them figure out exactly the right calculations, which IRS tables they should use, and making sure they stay on the right track and don't end up with a tax penalty. I believe that's what makes me different, and that's what makes our firm different.

Step 2: Income Planning and Analysis

Step two in our Retirement Roadmap 3-Step Review process is doing a retirement income analysis. When we survey folks nearing retirement, the No. 1 concern people have is running out of money. One of the most important things we can help you do is build a comprehensive written retirement income plan and do an analysis of what you have, so you can go to bed at night knowing we've built a retirement income plan that will give you a high probability of maintaining your lifestyle throughout your retirement.

Historically, there was something called the three-legged stool in retirement. The three-legged stool meant that in retirement, you would have income from three different places that added up to enough stable, predictable income for you to maintain your lifestyle through retirement. The first leg of the stool was Social Security, which, fortunately, is still around. I believe with some adjustments from Congress over the years, it should be sustainable.

The second leg of the stool was an employer pension. When I survey clients who attend my workshops, I find fewer and fewer retirees these days have the security of an employer pension to combine with their Social Security.

The third leg of the stool was your own savings and investments. Those can include your 401(k), 403(b), IRA, and Roth IRA.

If more and more employees are retiring without employer pension plans, can Social Security make up the difference, or will you make up the difference with your own savings and retirement? That's the more likely scenario as the cost of living adjustments on Social Security remains relatively low each year.

I sat down with two prospective clients, Bill and Connie. Bill and Connie had just retired and were proud when they came in. They had both turned 66, which is full retirement age based on their year of birth. I asked Bill what his Social Security was, and he told me $2,500 per month. When I asked Connie what hers was, she said $750 per month. They were both proud they had started to receive those benefits about a month earlier when they had filed.

I said, "Wait a minute, there's something wrong here. Connie, do you understand that the way the Social Security rules are drafted, you are entitled to half of Bill's Social Security or your own earnings record of $750; whichever is greater? Bill is now receiving $2,500 a month. You should be receiving at least $1,250 per month because half of his benefit is greater than your own."

Connie looked at me with disbelief and said, "we always thought our benefits were based on our own earnings record."

I said, "they are, except for spouses. The spouse with the lower income always has the ability to collect half the higher earning spouse's benefit if it's greater than their own. After you leave this appointment today, I want you to go down to Social Security, set an appointment, and have them recalculate your benefit."

A couple weeks later, Connie called me and thanked me, saying her first check for $1,250 had just posted to her bank account and that I was her new favorite person. She received a difference of $500 a month; a 40% increase in her monthly benefit. The average life for a female is 85 years, so that could mean $120,000 more for Connie over her life expectancy.

The reason Social Security didn't point this out to her is she had filed online, and Social Security is not designed to give you advice on what the best claiming strategy is for you. In fact, Social Security specifically limits the level of financial advice their support desk is allowed to offer. It's important you work with a qualified retirement planner, who can help run the analysis, including a Social Security analysis, to give you the steps you may want to take to claim and receive maximum benefits over your life expectancy.

Whether you are collecting or haven't started collecting yet, when you meet with us, you'll received a complimentary Social Security analyzer report to help you make the right decisions for your situation.

One of the largest studies to date on retirement vulnerability was done by Ernst and Young in all 50 states[4]. They surveyed folks who were seven years before retirement all the way to folks who were retiring. In the state of Arizona, they found that 8 of 10 new retirees without an employer pension plan are likely to outlive their assets. That's 80% of those 10,000 Baby Boomers per day or 8,000 of 10,000 per day likely to outlive their assets if they don't have employer pension plans.

The research also found that married couples are more likely to outlive their financial assets due to longer joint life spans. All the bickering keeps you alive longer! That's a joke I like to make.

Additionally, it found that single women run the highest risk of running out of money; higher than single men. The reason for that includes three factors. First is pay inequity. Women are not paid fairly. In the United States, the average is 80 cents on the dollar[5], and for minority women, the disparity is even worse. The second factor is time off to raise children, which results in fewer earned credits toward Social Security benefits and fewer paychecks to defer a portion of income into a retirement plan. Finally, there's genetics. On average, women live four to five years longer than men. When you have a longer life expectancy, you save less money and have fewer Social Security benefits. This puts single women at the greatest risk of running out of money in retirement.

If you're a single woman, what can you do about it? If you don't have an employer pension plan or a significant pension plan, you can take a portion of your retirement savings and buy your own pension utilizing a type of fixed annuity.

You'll want to be careful in this marketplace because there are a variety of annuity products out there. For retirement planning, depending on your particular situation, I prefer to use fixed or fixed index annuities only. I have found these types of accounts provide higher levels of guaranteed income at lower costs and without the risk of stock market declines affecting the income stream.

I recently worked with a client named Carol. The 55-year-old living in north Scottsdale had saved very well for retirement. She had $1 million saved for retirement, which is great at her age. The average for a 55-year-old is much less than that. When we built out Carol's retirement income plan, we figured she would work until age 65 and then retire. She wanted to have $100,000 of stable, predictable income before taxes at age 65. We also built a plan so her home would be paid off by that point. Her Social Security and her small employer pension added up to $40,000 a year at age 65.

We shopped the marketplace for different fixed annuity carriers to buy her a steady, predictable income stream starting at age 65 at $60,000 a year. When we shopped the marketplace at that time, we found we needed to use $576,000 of her $1 million to accomplish her goal. This would keep $424,000 in her investment portfolios and 10 more years of her working and saving to build her portfolio back up, which could also be used to offset her cost of living in the future. Carol's portfolio was decimated during the financial crisis of 2008 and 2009 and she didn't want to live through that again, worrying about not having enough money to maintain her lifestyle through retirement.

Keeping in mind the three-legged stool, even though Carol had a very small employer pension, she was able to take some of her own savings and investments and buy her own pension-style income utilizing a fixed annuity, which, when coupled with her additional Social Security benefit, would give her the stable, predictable income she needed at 65 to maintain her lifestyle throughout retirement while still having full liquidity of the remaining portfolio assets.

This was important to Carol for other reasons too. Carol's mother lives in Sun City, AZ, and she's 88 years old. Carol's aunt also lives in Sun City, and she's 92 years old. Carol's grandmother lived to the age of 101, so Carol knows she has significant longevity in her family.

Her guaranteed lifetime income annuity will generate $60,000 a year, every year, starting at age 65. If we do the math on that, it checks out like this: from 65 to 75, her annuity will have paid her $600,000. She made an initial deposit of $576,000. After she lives from 75 to 85, her annuity will have paid her $1.2 million. If she lives from 85 to 95, her annuity will have paid her $1.8 million guaranteed, regardless of what the stock market does during those time periods.

Most people don't have a process or somebody qualified to take them through all those steps, so they can make the right decisions about Social Security based on their situation; figure out all the legs of the three-legged stool; figure out how to make sure they have pension-style income, even if they don't have it from their employer; ensure they make the right decisions about Social Security; and manage the rest of their savings, investments, and retirement. That's what makes our firm different.

Step 3: Risk Exposure Evaluation

Step three in our Retirement Roadmap 3-Step Review process is our risk and fee analysis section. We talked about fees earlier with the shopping cart analogy. Now let's talk about risk.

When I ask the typical retiree, "what do you think the average return of the S&P 500 Index has been from the turn of the century, January of 2000, through the end of 2016?" I usually hear answers like 6%, 8%, or 10% per year. Then I pull up a chart from Google Finance that shows the actual annualized return, excluding dividends, was about 3% during that 17-year timeframe.

There were also two significant events that happened then; what we might call "black-swan" events: the dot.com crash from 2000 to 2002 had a 47% draw down on the S&P 500 from the highest point to the lowest point, and then the market recovered until the high of Oct. 9, 2007 when the housing market crashed. The S&P 500 declined 57% from the highest point to the lowest point.

When you plan for retirement, if you leave all your money in a portfolio that's passive and moving with the whims of the stock market, it can be very difficult to generate stable, predictable income. If the market is going down, you still need your income per month to live on.

Therefore, when you're building a retirement income plan, you usually want to make sure that the stable, predictable income you need for retirement is coming from guaranteed income sources: pensions, annuities, Social Security. Then you want to ensure that the remaining assets are in a properly allocated portfolio. I choose to use TD Ameritrade's institutional platform for my clients. It's the best low-cost platform I have found that can provide quality asset-management services with the ability to minimize holdings in both equities and fixed income during periods of decline.

Think of it as going down a steep mountain road. On the side of the road, there are guard rails. When you're hiring a portfolio-management team, you should ask if they have some sort of guard rails. In our language, that's tactical monitoring: daily monitoring to be able to change the investments or go to cash or a fixed income on portions of the portfolio to minimize the draw down during the inevitable next market cycle. Most people don't have a process to figure out how to choose the right investments in their portfolio; the investments that give them that layer of tactical monitoring to help minimize exposure to major stock-market events while still potentially maximizing growth potential and minimizing fees and taxes. That's what makes our firm different.

Estate Planning

Many of our clients utilize the estate planning attorney we work with to review, update, and create solid estate plans that coordinate all their assets, making sure the titling of those assets and real estate or business interests is done properly, and ensure all of the beneficiary forms in all their accounts are filled out correctly.

There are three basic ways to plan your estate. When I speak with our attorney, this is one of the examples he gives. You can do nothing, which is the most popular estate planning tool available today. More than 50% of Americans have no estate plan in place, which means if they die, they die in a process called intestate. That means there's an automatic probate process over the assets because there was no will or trust in place.

The second most popular planning tool is a last will and testament. A will is sufficient in certain cases. In the state of Arizona, you can pass up to $100,000 of real estate equity with a will without going through probate. Probate is the court process that assets stuck in a deceased person's name need to go through to get unstuck and distributed properly to the heirs.

A will is not a legal way of avoiding the probate process if the equity in the asset exceeds $100,000 (as of the time this book was written). That's why many families nearing retirement choose to structure a revocable living trust.

While it may not be appropriate for all, a revocable living trust is a transparent legal entity that becomes the new title holder to one's assets. You're getting things out of your name and putting them in your trust's name. The trust has a series of managers called trustees who can make decisions about which assets are in the trust and how they're to be administered.

The benefit of doing that is if the original creators become incapacitated or pass away, they control who the next person in charge is; the person who will make decisions on their behalf; rather than losing control to the court system.

Make sure you have your estate plan up to date. There are usually four core documents retirees need to have: the revocable living trust, the pour over will, powers of attorney (including medical, financial, and mental healthcare power of attorney), and a living will that discusses life support. I can't emphasize this enough: make sure you have a properly funded estate plan and are working with a qualified advisor and qualified estate planning attorney to review and draft the documents. Keep the lawyers and courts out of your estate. Draft the proper documents, fund the assets properly, and make sure you have all the beneficiaries checked properly in order to do that. What makes us different is that we help you get and stay organized, and we keep a copy of all those documents in your estate planning binder.

Investment Advisors vs. Brokers

Who is giving you financial advice? For the majority of the last 50 years, most people who got financial advice got it from somebody who is considered a stockbroker. That doesn't mean the advice was bad; it just means the advice came from someone who had not been held to a fiduciary standard. Fewer advisors, myself and my team included, are licensed as investment advisor representatives, which makes them a fiduciary on behalf of the client.

Why is this important? A fiduciary is legally obligated to place the client's interest first. When you're planning for retirement, you want to make sure you work with somebody who puts your needs first — somebody who is paid based on giving you advice; who's transparent; and, if they're managing assets for you, somebody who is fee-based rather than commission-based.

As of the writing of this book, this is a hot topic. The Department of Labor issued the fiduciary standard rule, which seeks to apply the fiduciary standard to all financial advice-givers, including brokers. That rule is undergoing a review and may not be implemented on
Jan. 1, 2018 in its current form.

In the meantime, you can seek out an advisor who is already a fiduciary; somebody who has a process to help you uncover all the critical facts necessary for you to make sound decisions about your retirement. You want somebody who can help you put your entire financial house in order, including your income plan, investment plan, tax plan, long-term healthcare plan, and estate plan.

When I think about the challenges my own mom and dad experienced because they didn't have somebody to go to for retirement planning, I wish that I had been further along in my career as they entered retirement. Research conducted by the Retirement Research Consortium at the Wharton School found those who worked with qualified advisors ended up with three times as much money in retirement as those who didn't, on average[6]. Here are five critical questions to ask any financial advisor:

*Have you adequately reviewed my personal financial situation to make sure this recommendation is in my best interest?

*How will your plan impact my tax return each year and what future tax issues may concern me?

*How will your plan affect my income and liquidity needs in the future?

*How does your plan match up with my risk comfort level?

*How will your plan affect the transition of my estate to my heirs?

When you come in, we'll take you through our Retirement Roadmap 3-Step Review process. My team will give you a list of things to bring in, and we'll draft out your written retirement income plan, having done the analysis of your retirement plan. We will do the risk and fee analysis, and we'll look at decisions about Social Security. You'll also receive our 2017 key data card, which includes all the information for making sound decisions from a tax perspective for 2017, as well as a copy of my book, *Climbing the Retirement Mountain.*

To get started, you can call my office at **602-343-9301** to schedule a consultation or email **Advisors@StrategyFinancialGroup.com**. You can also visit **StrategyFinancialGroup.com**.

How to Maintain Your Financial Independence Through Retirement and Live Your Best Life

You may already know that minimizing taxes and maintaining a retirement income stream that is sustainable for the rest of your life are the two most important factors that will affect the quality of your retirement, but do you understand all of the different tax rules and income generating vehicles available in the marketplace so that you can make the right decisions for your retirement? That's where we come in. We help retirees just like you create your retirement roadmap to maintain your financial independence through retirement.

Step 1: We start by reviewing your 1040 tax returns. We will drill down on the critical areas to minimize your taxes. This means you will have more money for travel, dining out, and home improvement projects rather than giving it to the IRS!

Step 2: We develop a retirement income analysis and comprehensive written retirement income plan. This means you can finally put to rest your concerns about running out of money.

Step 3: A comprehensive Risk & Fee Analysis to find ways to minimize fees and expenses in your portfolio. This means we will help you invest defensively so that your retirement plans are not derailed by the next market downturn.

After implementing the recommendations at the end of our three-step review process, we meet to check in on the overall plan and make sure we're on track with any changes that may have occurred in your life.

Most people are unaware of the retirement tax loopholes that exist that can help leave more money in their pocket so they can travel more, spend more time with grandchildren and have a greater sense of financial independence.

Now you can map your road to retirement and live your best life in retirement.

Get started today by calling **602-343-9301 or email Advisors@StrategyFinancialGroup.com** to schedule your Retirement Roadmap 3-Step Review.

[1] Hill, Patrick L., Turiano, Nicholas A. *Purpose in Life as a Predictor of Mortality Across Adulthood,* Psycological Science, (2014)

[2] R Edelen, R Evans, G Kadlec *Shedding light on "invisible" costs: Trading costs and mutual fund performance*- Financial Analysts Journal, 2013 - CFA Institute

[3] Williams, S. (2016, June 27) *Here's How Much the Average American Has in an IRA, Sorted by Age.* Retrieved from http://www.fool.com/retirement

[4] Plumb, T. (2008, July 14) Study: Most middle-class retirees will outlive retirement savings. Retrieved from https://www.bizjournals.com

[5] Gould, E., Schieder, J., Geier, K. (2016, October 20) What is the gender pay gap and is it real? Retrieved from www.epi.org

[6] Annamaria Lusardi & Olivia S. Mitchell, 2011. "Financial Literacy and Planning: Implications for Retirement Wellbeing," NBER Working Papers 17078, National Bureau of Economic Research, Inc.

Made in the USA
Middletown, DE
23 December 2021

56807008R00027